§ ANCIENT WORLDS ॐ

WAGING ANCIENT WARFARE

Martin Gitlin

45th Parallel Press

Published in the United States of America by Cherry Lake Publishing Group
Ann Arbor, Michigan
www.cherrylakepublishing.com

Reading Adviser: Beth Walker Gambro, MS, Ed., Reading Consultant, Yorkville, IL

Photo Credits: © David C Azor/Shutterstock, cover, title page; Public Domain, MS Am 1371.6. Houghton Library, Harvard University, 4; © Avesun/Shutterstock, 7; © PHILIP WILLS/Shutterstock, 8; © 3DF mediaStudio/Shutterstock, 10; Johannes Meursius, CC0, via Wikimedia Commons, 12; © Vasileios Karafillidis/Shutterstock, 15; © WH_Pics/Shutterstock, 16; © Begir/Shutterstock, 18; Ma Lin, Public domain, via Wikimedia Commons, 20; Gary Todd from Xinzheng, China, CC0, via Wikimedia Commons, 23; © Oleksandr Rostunov/Shutterstock, 24; © Oguz Dikbakan/Shutterstock, 26; © PRISMA ARCHIVO/Alamy Stock Photo, 28; Internet Archive Book Images, No restrictions, via Wikimedia Commons, 30

Graphic Element Credits: Graphic Element Credits: Cover, multiple interior pages: © Andrey_Kuzmin/Shutterstock, © cajoer/Shutterstock, © GUSAK OLENA/Shutterstock, © Eky Studio/Shutterstock

Copyright © 2025 by Cherry Lake Publishing Group
All rights reserved. No part of this book may be reproduced or utilized
in any form or by any means without written permission from the publisher.
45TH Parallel Press is an imprint of Cherry Lake Publishing Group.

Library of Congress Cataloging-in-Publication Data has been filed and is available at catalog.loc.gov.

Cherry Lake Publishing Group would like to acknowledge the work of the Partnership for 21st Century Learning, a Network of Battelle for Kids. Please visit http://www.battelleforkids.org/networks/p21 for more information.

Printed in the United States of America

Note from publisher: Websites change regularly, and their future contents are outside of our control. Supervise children when conducting any recommended online searches for extended learning opportunities.

About the Author
Martin Gitlin is an educational book author based in Connecticut. He won more than 45 awards as a newspaper journalist from 1991 to 2002. Included was a first-place award from the Associated Press. That organization voted him as one of the top four feature writers in Ohio in 2002. Martin has had about 250 books published since 2006. Most of them were written for students. He has authored many books about history.

TABLE OF CONTENTS

Introduction 4

Chapter 1: Mayhem in Mesopotamia 8

Chapter 2: A Phony Trojan Horse 12

Chapter 3: Chariots of War 16

Chapter 4: The Battles to Dominate China 20

Chapter 5: The Catapult 24

Chapter 6: Greek Fire 28

Glossary 32
Learn More 32
Index 32

INTRODUCTION

George Santayana is a philosopher. He warned that those who don't learn from history are doomed to repeat it. He said this in 1905.

Some things never change. That includes human behavior. Thousands of years have passed. Conflict remains. People fight. So do nations. Leaders can't keep peace. So they declare war. Soldiers are killed. So are **civilians**. These are people who are not in the armed forces. No one wins in war.

Humans must learn from history. They must not repeat mistakes. They must study wars. They must know its horrors. People die in war. Cities are destroyed. Many suffer. But war goes on. The same evils are repeated.

It was no different in ancient times. Rulers fought for power. They battled for land. They formed armies. Ancient wars have been studied. Research goes back 5,000 years. People know the causes of wars. But they don't know how to stop wars.

Modern wars are more dangerous. Weapons are deadlier. They kill in greater numbers. Ancient wars had no bombs. They had no guns. They started as hand-to-hand combat. People used **primitive** weapons. Primitive means basic and simple.

What caused ancient wars? How did they start? That remains unchanged. The cause is about power. People kill to get it. Rulers want to grow their lands. They attack other lands. Or civil wars begin. Groups of people want to dominate others. People resist.

Ancient wars changed the world. They altered the balance of power. Empires arose. Nations grew. War helped some people thrive. Others suffered. Many died. Rulers gained fame. They gained wealth. So did military leaders. Some were hated. Some were loved.

The 2 deadliest ancient wars were in China. Millions died.

CHAPTER ONE

Kish was a kingdom in Sumer.

Mayhem in Mesopotamia

Wars may have been fought before 2700 BCE. But nobody knows for sure. None were recorded. War history starts in Mesopotamia. That is modern-day Iran and Iraq. War revolved around 2 countries. The countries were Sumer and Elam. Sumer recorded battle outcomes.

Experts have different ideas about ancient wars. Some claim it was over trade routes. Others claim it was over farmland. People were no longer hunters and gatherers. They had become farmers. They wanted plots of land. They needed to grow food.

Early fights were simple. Small groups of people fought. They used primitive weapons. Fights became more advanced. Soldiers used swords. They used shields.

Enmebaragesi was king of Sumer. He was a key leader. He wanted to expand his rule. So Sumer attacked Elam. Elam was a new country. Sumer's victory was easy.

Sumer trained soldiers. These soldiers were placed in **units**. Units are organized groups. These units practiced **formations**. Formations are military movements. Sumer's soldiers had new weapons.

Sumer was more prepared. It seized Elam's weapons. It took over its forces. It gained power. It won the war. Elam had no chance.

Sumer's soldiers protected their heads. They wore helmets. The helmets were made of copper and bronze.

A NICE STORY

Not all ancient war heroes were men. There were women war heroes. The Trung sisters lived in ancient Vietnam. Starting in 111 BCE, China invaded north Vietnam. It wanted more land and power. Vietnamese women had more rights than Chinese women.

Trung Trac and Trung Nhi were sisters. They were born in the early 1st century CE. They were highly educated. Their father was a military leader. The Chinese killed Trac's husband. Trac was mad. She and her sister raised an army. They led 80,000 soldiers. They led the army into battle. They resisted Chinese rule. They fought for freedom. They defeated the Chinese. They saved Vietnam.

Trac became the first female Vietnamese ruler. Nhi was her top advisor. They ruled over 65 cities. Years later, the Chinese attacked again. The Trung sisters met their armies. They rode elephants. They lost this battle. But they're fondly remembered. There's a temple named after them. The Vietnamese people still honor them.

Ancient people believed Homer's poems were true stories. This is because they included conversations and speeches.

A Phony Trojan Horse

Did the Trojan War happen? Was the Trojan horse story true? Were they myths? Or were they real? This has been debated for years.

It was true to ancient Greeks. That view came from Homer. Homer was a poet. He wrote 2 famous poems. One was *The Iliad*. The other was *The Odyssey*. Both poems described the Trojan War. The Greeks fought the Trojans. Agamemnon was king of Mycenae. He led the Greek troops. The Trojan leader was Priam.

The poems gave great details. They claim Paris sparked the war. Paris was Priam's son. He said Aphrodite was the most beautiful goddess. She gave him a gift. The gift was Helen.

Agamemnon's brother was married to Helen. Agamemnon got mad. He declared war on Troy. The Greeks won.

Did the poems reflect real life? Ancient historians thought so. They wrote about it years later. But modern experts deny it. They also deny its most famous story. That was about the Trojan horse.

The tale is told in *The Odyssey*. Greece had fought Troy for 10 years. The Greeks couldn't get inside the gates of Troy. They formed a plan. They hid in a huge wooden horse. The horse was outside the gates. The Trojans thought the Greeks had left. They pulled in the horse. That night, the Greeks sneaked out of the horse. They had been hiding inside. They opened the gates. Greek armies rushed into Troy. The Trojans were surprised. This Greek attack ended the war.

Was it all a myth? Some believe the war happened. But they doubt the Trojan horse story.

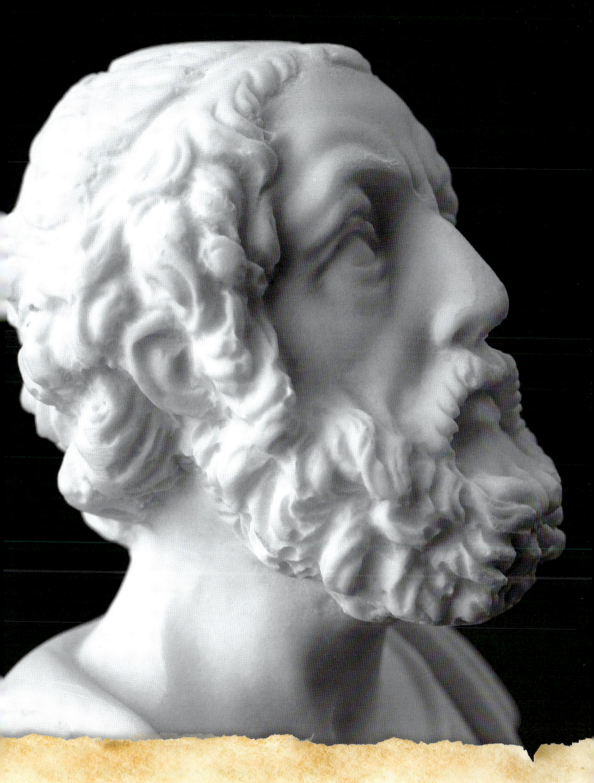

Some doubt Homer even existed. His poems were made before works were written down. There is no other proof of him.

CHAPTER THREE

Battering rams were used. They smashed through castle gates. They were used in a Persian war. This happened around 400 BCE.

Chariots of War

Soldiers need speed. Modern jets can fly up to 4,500 miles (7,242 kilometers) per hour. Tanks move fast.

The earliest soldiers fought on foot. Then came carts. They were slow. Soon **chariots** were invented. Chariots are 2-wheeled carts. They are pulled by animals. They changed warfare. They increased speed for soldiers. Soldiers could attack faster. Combat was never the same.

That was not always true. Chariots were invented around 3000 BCE. At first, they were slow. They were bulky. They were unfit for combat. That changed 1,000 years later. Lighter chariots were built. They became weapons.

The speedy chariots won wars. They drove circles around enemies. Troops shot arrows from them. Their arrows flew far. The chariots kept the soldiers safe. Soldiers stayed out of range. Soldiers on foot couldn't reach them.

Armies on chariots organized in formations. They charged the enemy. The result was deadly. They became powerful. They attacked other lands. They dominated wars. They swallowed territories. Empires were built. Among them was the Greek empire. The world changed.

But chariots faded as a combat tool. This happened around 500 BCE. They became too expensive. They moved poorly on rough land. Each required 2 men. One man shot weapons. The other had to drive. Chariots were phased out.

The ancient Romans used chariots for racing. They didn't use them for warfare.

MYSTERY SOLVED OR UNSOLVED?

Much is known about great ancient rulers. Written history details their lives. It explains military conquests. But where are they buried? Not much is known.

That is true of Mark Antony. He was a Roman general. He was defeated in 31 BCE at the Battle of Actium. He then stabbed himself. He used his sword. Cleopatra was his lover. She was queen of ancient Egypt. She also killed herself. Books and plays were written about their lives. But their burial sites remain a mystery. Some think it's in Alexandria. That was in Egypt. That city was lost to a storm in 365 CE. Others think they're buried along the Nile River. They claim their tombs are in a temple.

Alexandria was named after Alexander the Great. He was a Greek king. His burial site is also a mystery. So is that of Genghis Khan. Khan was a harsh Mongol ruler. He built an empire in Central Asia. But nobody is sure where he's buried.

CHAPTER FOUR

This is King Wu of Zhou. He hated King Di Xin of Shang.

The Battles to Dominate China

Ancient China was not a country. It was a group of states. There were power struggles. **Dynasties** ruled. Dynasties are ruling families. Wars were common. Soldiers rode horseback. They clashed with swords. They shot deadly arrows. Combat shaped Chinese history.

The Battle of Muye was fought in 1046 BCE. One side fought for King Wu of Zhou. The other sided with King Di Xin of Shang. The Shang Dynasty was brutal. Wu wanted to defeat it.

The battle proved that bigger armies can lose. Di Xin had 170,000 troops. Wu had 50,000. But Wu's men had more passion. Di Xin used enslaved people. They didn't want to fight. Many rebelled. King Di Xin of Shang was beaten. Some say he torched his palace. They say he died in the fire.

It was 208 CE. The Han Dynasty was nearly over. Cao Cao was a warlord. He controlled northern China. He wanted more. He aimed to unify China under his rule. So he attacked.

Sun Quan and Liu Bei were ready. They were southern warlords. Their armies were much smaller. The battle was fought near the Red Cliffs. These cliffs were near the Yangtze River. Sun and Liu used strategy. They sent in ships. They told Cao Cao they were giving up. But they lied. The ships were filled with **flammable** material. Flammable means easily set on fire. Cao Cao's fleet was chained together. His ships caught fire. His forces were soon defeated.

Another smaller army had won. Strategy had again beaten size. Cao Cao retreated. The Three Kingdoms era began. Cao Cao, Liu, and Sun all ruled parts of China.

The Battle of Guandu was in 200 CE. Cao Cao took over northern China. He had a smaller army. He defeated Yuan Shao, a rival warlord.

CHAPTER FIVE

Catapults were used in warfare up through World War I (1914–1918).

The Catapult

Chariots were used for years. Then the **catapult** came along. It became a weapon of choice. Catapults are machines. They shoot or launch things.

It was around 400 BCE. Dionysius the Elder sought a new weapon. He was a Greek **tyrant**. This is a harsh ruler. They have a lot of power. He invented the catapult. It worked in warfare. It could throw 350-pound (160 kilograms) stones. And it could toss them 300 feet (91 meters).

Two catapult types were built. One had two arms. It shot arrows. The other had one arm. It shot huge rocks. The Romans added wheels. They could move them more easily. But designs changed little. Catapults stayed a weapon of choice.

Armies used catapults in the Middle Ages. People lived in walled cities. New uses had arrived. Soldiers set things on fire. Then catapults launched them.

Defensive strategy improved. Castles became better protected.

Catapults stayed around. They were even used in World War I (1914–1918). They tossed hand grenades. Those blew up near enemy **trenches**. But the catapult was no longer a major weapon of war.

This is an example of a one-armed catapult.

ANCIENT RULES

The *Mahabharata* is the longest poem ever. It has nearly 2 million words. It was written in ancient India. Some parts describe the Kurukshetra War.

The poem includes rules of war. Here are some of them:

- Fighting must begin no earlier than sunrise. And it should end no later than sunset.
- Multiple warriors must not attack one warrior.
- Warriors doing battle must use the same weapons. They must also be on the same mount. Included are elephants and chariots.
- Prisoners of war must be protected.
- No warriors who surrender can be killed.
- Unarmed warriors cannot be harmed or killed.
- Civilians and animals must be kept safe.
- No warrior may kill or harm another whose back is turned.

Nearly all those rules were broken. And the war lasted only 18 days.

The Greeks kept their fire mixture a secret. Its ingredients remain unknown today.

Greek Fire

The Greeks didn't invent fire. But they sure used it. And not just to cook food. It helped them win wars.

They mixed flammable ingredients. The mixture caught fire. The Greeks gained fame for it. It was known as "Greek fire."

Callinicus of Heliopolis invented Greek fire. He was a Syrian **refugee**. Refugees flee from their countries. The Greeks fired flaming arrows. They flung firepots. The weapons were launched from tubes. They were shot from ships.

The Greeks dominated naval warfare. **Naval** refers to warships. Navies are used to fight in water. They travel by ship.

The Arabs struck Constantinople in 673 CE. That was the capital of the Byzantine Empire. But the Greeks stopped them. Greek fire was special. It couldn't be put out with water. It destroyed Arab fleets.

Historians wrote much about Greek fire. It made a loud roar. It made smoke. It made enemies flee. There was only 1 way to put it out. A special mixture was made. It had sand, vinegar, and old pee!

Some think that petroleum and sulfur were used to make Greek fire.

VERY IMPORTANT PEOPLE

Weapons of war have changed the world. But someone had to invent them. Among the most creative was Archimedes. He was a Greek inventor. He created a weapon named after him. It was the Claw of Archimedes.

The ancient machine was strange. It looked like a crane. It was installed along the sea. It defended Syracuse. Syracuse was a Greek city. The claw stopped sea attacks before they started. The machine had a rope. It had a gripping hook.

A lever pushed the claw into action. It was launched as attacking ships came close. The claw gripped the ship. Then it raised the ship. That caused great damage. The claw could lift a ship out of the water. That action shook the ship. Every man aboard would be tossed into the water. The ship then sank.

GLOSSARY

catapult (KA-tuh-puhlt) a machine that can throw something with great force

chariots (CHAIR-ee-uhts) carts with 2 wheels pulled by animals

civilians (suh-VIL-yunz) people who are not in the armed forces

dynasties (DIYE-nuh-steez) rulers or families that maintain power for a long time

flammable (FLA-muh-buhl) something that easily catches fire

formations (for-MAY-shuhnz) positions or movements in which armed soldiers enter and fight battles

naval (NAY-vuhl) related to warships or the navy forces

primitive (PRIM-ih-tiv) related to an early age or period in history

refugee (re-FYOO-jee) a person who flees a country to escape danger

trenches (TRENCH-iz) long ditches usually used for military purposes

tyrant (TYE-runt) a harsh person or leader who has absolute power

units (YOO-nuhts) organized groups of soldiers

LEARN MORE

Jones, Gareth, ed. *Military History: The Definitive Visual Guide to the Objects of Warfare*. New York: DK, 2015.

Rhoderick, Ryan. *Greatest Battles for Boys: The Ancient Wars*. Quebec, Canada: Lexah Publications, 2022.

Search online with an adult:
National Geographic Kids: 10 Facts about Ancient Greece

INDEX

Agamemnon, 13–14
Archimedes, 31
armies, 11, 14, 18, 21–23

burials of rulers, 19

Cao Cao, 22–23
catapults, 24–26
causes of war, 5–6, 9, 11, 13–14, 21–22
chariots, 17–18, 25, 27
China, 7, 11, 20–23
civilians, 5, 27
consequences of war, 5–7, 18

dynasties, 21–23

Greece, 13–14, 18, 19, 25, 28–31
Greek fire, 28–30

Helen of Troy, 13–14
historians, 5, 14, 30
Homer, 12–15

innovations in warfare, 6, 9–10, 17–18, 24–26, 28–31

land, 5–6, 9, 11, 18

Mesopotamia, 8–10
military leaders, 6, 10, 11, 19, 22–23

military strategy, 10, 14, 18, 22–23, 26
modern warfare, 5–6, 17, 24, 26

naval warfare, 22, 30–31

The Odyssey (Homer), 13–14

power, 5–6, 10, 11,18, 21–22

Rome, 18, 19, 25
rulers, 5, 6, 11, 13, 19, 20–23, 25
rules of war, 27

ships, 22, 29–31
soldiers, 5, 9–10, 11, 17–18, 21, 26
Sumer (Kish), 8–10

Trojan Horse and War, 13–14
Trung sisters, 11

victories in war, 10, 11, 14, 21–23, 30

weapons, 6, 9, 10, 16–18, 21, 22, 24–26, 27, 28–31